D1379363

Farmyard Friends

CHICKENS

Maddie Gibbs

PowerKiDS
press.

New York

Published in 2015 by The Rosen Publishing Group, Inc.
29 East 21st Street, New York, NY 10010

First Edition

Editor: Caitie McAneney
Book Design: Katelyn Heinle

Photo Credits: Cover, p. 1 Jon Beard/Shutterstock.com; p. 5 Jordan Tan/Shutterstock.com; pp. 6, 24 (rooster) PCHT/ Shutterstock.com; p. 9 Nataliia Melnychuk/Shutterstock.com; p. 10 BestPhotoPlus/Shutterstock.com; p. 13 John Panella/Shutterstock.com; p. 14 Kemeo/Shutterstock.com; p. 17 wavebreakmedia/Shutterstock.com; p. 18 Amy Kerkemeyer/Shutterstock.com; p. 21 cynoclub/Shutterstock.com; p. 22 holbox/Shutterstock.com; p. 24 (vegetables) Symbiot/Shutterstock.com.

Library of Congress Cataloging-in-Publication Data

Gibbs, Maddie, author.
 Chickens / Maddie Gibbs.
     pages cm. — (Farmyard friends)
 Includes index.
 ISBN 978-1-4994-0066-3 (pbk.)
 ISBN 978-1-4994-0069-4 (6 pack)
 ISBN 978-1-4994-0064-9 (library binding)
 1. Chickens—Juvenile literature. 2. Domestic animals—Juvenile literature. I. Title.
 SF487.5.G55 2015
 636.5—dc23
                                        2014025273

Manufactured in the United States of America

CPSIA Compliance Information: Batch #CW15PK: For Further Information contact Rosen Publishing, New York, New York at 1-800-237-9932

CONTENTS

Many farms have chickens.
Chickens are raised for food
all over the world!

comb

wattle

Roosters are male chickens. Roosters have a **comb** on their head. They have a **wattle** on their chin.

A female chicken is called a hen. A hen lays about 300 eggs every year.

Baby chickens are called chicks.
They break out of eggs.

Most farm chickens live
in pens called coops.

Farmers feed chickens seeds, **vegetables**, and grain. They love bugs and worms, too!

Farmers raise chickens
for their eggs and meat.
They also make great pets!

Plymouth Rock chickens have striped feathers. They first came from America.

Silkie chickens are very fluffy. They're also friendly and fun to watch!

Chickens don't just live on farms. You can keep them in your backyard!

WORDS TO KNOW

comb

vegetables

wattle

INDEX

WEBSITES

Due to the changing nature of Internet links, PowerKids Press has developed an online list of websites related to the subject of this book. This site is updated regularly. Please use this link to access the list: www.powerkidslinks.com/fmyd/chic